10 SMART MONEY MOVES

Building Money Lessons for Teens and Young Adults

By

JORDAN WISEBERG

Title: 10 Smart Money Moves: Building Money Lessons for Teens and Young Adults

Author: Jordan Wiseberg

ISBN: 9798856119120

Imprint: Independently published

Disclaimer: The information provided in this book is for educational purposes only and does not constitute financial advice. The author and publisher are not responsible for any actions taken based on the content of this book. Readers should consult with a qualified financial advisor before making any financial decisions.

ACKNOWLEDGMENTS

I would like to express my deepest gratitude to all those who have contributed to the creation of this book, "10 Smart Money Moves: Building Money Lessons for Teens and Young Adults."

First and foremost, I want to thank my family for their unwavering support and encouragement throughout this journey. Your belief in me and my passion for financial education has been a constant source of motivation.

To my friends and colleagues who provided valuable insights and feedback, thank you for your time and thoughtful contributions. Your perspectives enriched the content of this book and helped shape its message.

I am also indebted to the experts and professionals in the field of personal finance who generously shared their knowledge and expertise. Your guidance has been instrumental in ensuring the accuracy and relevance of the financial lessons presented in this book.

To the readers and young adults who will embark on their financial journeys with the help of this book, thank you for your interest and willingness to learn. It is my hope that the lessons shared here will empower you to make smart money moves and build a strong financial future.

Lastly, I want to extend my appreciation to the countless individuals who have worked behind the scenes to make this book a reality. Your dedication and commitment to producing a high-quality publication are truly commendable.

To all those who have played a part, big or small, in the creation of "10 Smart Money Moves," thank you from the bottom of my heart.

Sincerely,

Jordan Wiseberg

Table of Content

INTRODUCTION

In a small town called Prosperityville, lived two best friends, Emma and Alex. They were teenagers with big dreams, just like any other young adults stepping into the world of possibilities. One sunny afternoon, as they strolled through the park, they stumbled upon an old, dusty book lying on a bench. The title read, *"10 Smart Money Moves: Building Money Lessons for Teens and Young Adults."* Curiosity got the better of them, and they decided to dive into its pages.

The book was like a treasure trove of financial wisdom, guiding them through the maze of money management with real-life stories, practical tips, and valuable lessons. Emma and Alex were instantly drawn to the captivating tales of young entrepreneurs, college fund wizards, and benevolent givers who had turned their financial struggles into inspiring success stories.

As they delved deeper into the chapters, they discovered the magic of budgeting, the power of saving and investing, and the art of making sound financial decisions. The book enlightened them about credit cards, loans, and the importance of building a strong credit score. It also opened their eyes to the significance of giving back to the community and creating a positive impact on the world.

With each turn of the page, Emma and Alex felt empowered and excited about their financial future. They realized that financial literacy was not just a concept for grown-ups but a vital tool for young individuals like them. The book provided them with the knowledge and confidence to take control of their finances, make informed choices, and set themselves on the path to financial independence.

As Emma and Alex implemented the smart money moves they learned, they witnessed remarkable changes in their lives. They saved money effortlessly, invested wisely, and planned ahead for college and their dreams. Their journey wasn't without challenges, but armed with the knowledge from the book, they navigated through financial hurdles with resilience and determination.

One day, as they were enjoying a cup of coffee at their favorite hangout spot, they noticed their friends, Kate and Mike, discussing their worries about money matters.

Remembering how the book had transformed their lives, Emma and Alex decided to share their newfound knowledge. They lent Kate and Mike the book, and just like Emma and Alex before them, they too became engrossed in its pages.

Seeing the positive impact the book had on their friends' lives, Emma and Alex realized that they had stumbled upon a hidden gem, a guide that could change the lives of countless teens and young adults who were struggling with financial decisions. They were determined to spread the word about "10 Smart Money Moves" to help others take charge of their financial destinies.

This e-book, "10 Smart Money Moves: Building Money Lessons for Teens and Young Adults," is the culmination of Emma and Alex's journey, their passion to empower others, and their desire to make a difference. It is a comprehensive guide filled with stories of real people who have achieved financial success and lessons that every young adult should know.

Dear reader, as you hold this book in your hands, we invite you to embark on a life-changing adventure.

Whether you are a teenager with dreams as vast as the sky or a young adult about to step into the world of financial independence, this book is designed to equip you with the essential money management skills you need to succeed.

Just like Emma and Alex, you will learn to budget like a pro, save and invest with purpose, understand credit cards and loans, build a strong credit score, and explore the power of giving back. You will discover how to make sound financial decisions, face challenges with confidence, and turn your dreams into reality.

Let the stories in these pages inspire you, the lessons empower you, and the knowledge guide you towards a future of financial prosperity. Your journey to financial independence starts here. Are you ready to make the Smart Money Moves that will shape your destiny? Let's begin!

Chapter One

Understanding the Basics of Money Management

Money management is the foundation of financial success. As a young adult, learning the art of managing your finances is crucial for a secure and prosperous future. In this chapter, we will explore the fundamental concepts of money management, including creating a personal budget, tracking expenses and income, understanding the importance of emergency savings, and finding the right balance between income and expenses.

The Concept of Money Management

Money management refers to the process of wisely handling your financial resources. It involves making informed decisions about how you earn, spend, save, and invest your money. At its core, money management is about setting financial goals, making a plan to achieve those goals, and staying disciplined in following that plan.

Effective money management starts with developing a clear understanding of your financial situation. Take the time to assess your income sources, such as allowances, part-time jobs, or money from family members. Next, identify your regular expenses, such as school-related costs, entertainment, and personal expenses. By having a comprehensive overview of your financial inflows and outflows, you can make better-informed decisions and avoid overspending.

Creating a Personal Budget

A personal budget is a useful tool that gives you financial control. It is a thorough plan that details your earnings and expenses for a given time frame, typically a month. It's important to carefully analyze your financial priorities and goals while making a budget.

To start, list all your sources of income. Whether it's from a part-time job or financial gifts, ensure you have a clear picture of the money coming in each month. Next, list your essential expenses, such as rent, utilities, and groceries. Allocating a portion of your income to savings and investments is equally important to secure your financial future.

Be realistic when budgeting for discretionary spending, such as entertainment and hobbies. While it's essential to enjoy life, overspending on non-essential items can lead to financial strain. Remember, a budget is a flexible tool that allows you to make adjustments as your circumstances change.

Tracking Expenses and Income

One of the most crucial aspects of money management is tracking your expenses and income. Often, we underestimate how much we spend on small, everyday purchases, which can add up significantly over time. By keeping a record of all your expenses, you'll gain insights into your spending habits and identify areas where you can cut back.

Numerous tools and apps are available to help you track your finances effectively. You can use spreadsheets, budgeting apps, or even a simple notebook. The key is to record every transaction accurately, from your morning coffee to larger expenses like textbooks or gadgets.

Tracking your income is equally important. Ensure that all your sources of income are recorded accurately, and cross-reference them with your budget. This way, you'll always know if you're living within your means or need to make adjustments to stay on track.

Importance of Emergency Savings

Because life is unpredictable, unexpected bills could occur at any time. That's where emergency savings come into play. Emergency savings are funds set aside to cover unforeseen expenses, such as medical emergencies, car repairs, or sudden job loss.

Having an emergency fund provides a safety net, protecting you from going into debt when unexpected challenges occur. As a general rule of thumb, aim to have at least three to six months' worth of living expenses in your emergency savings account.

Start building your emergency fund gradually. Over time, even modest efforts might add up. By setting up a direct deposit into a different savings account, you might want to think about automating your savings. This way, you won't be tempted to spend the money intended for emergencies.

Balancing Income and Expenses

Achieving financial stability requires finding the right balance between your income and expenses. It's essential to live within your means and avoid overspending, especially on non-essential items. Strive to save and invest a portion of your income regularly to build wealth over time.

Balancing your income and expenses also involves setting financial priorities. Determine what matters most to you, whether it's saving for college, traveling, or starting a business. By aligning your spending with your long-term goals, you'll be better equipped to make smart financial decisions.

Remember that achieving financial success is a journey, not an overnight accomplishment. Stay committed to your money management plan, continuously learn about personal finance, and seek guidance from trusted financial experts or mentors. By understanding the basics of money management and developing responsible financial habits, you are setting yourself up for a bright and financially secure future.

Developing Financial Discipline

Effective money management requires discipline and self-control. It's easy to be swayed by impulsive spending or the desire to keep up with friends who seem to have more disposable income. However, developing financial discipline is essential to avoid falling into debt and to build a strong financial foundation.

One way to cultivate financial discipline is to establish clear financial goals and remind yourself of these goals regularly. Having a vision of what you want to achieve financially will help you resist unnecessary expenses that may derail your plans.

Practice delayed gratification, which means resisting the urge to make spontaneous purchases and instead saving for things that truly matter to you. Consider whether a purchase aligns with your financial goals before making it. Often, you'll find that the excitement of immediate spending fades, but the satisfaction of reaching your long-term objectives endures.

Minimizing Debt

While some types of debt can be helpful, such as student loans for education or a reasonable mortgage for a home, excessive debt can become burdensome and hinder financial progress. High-interest debts, like credit card balances, can quickly spiral out of control if not managed carefully.

A key principle of money management is to minimize and manage debt responsibly. If you have outstanding debts, focus on paying them off systematically, starting with those carrying the highest interest rates. Create a debt repayment plan and commit to it diligently.

Avoid accumulating new debt unnecessarily. Use credit cards wisely and always aim to pay off the full balance each month to avoid interest charges. If you need to finance a purchase, explore alternatives like personal savings or zero-interest installment plans.

Cultivating Good Saving Habits

A key component of effective money management is saving. Saving provides financial security and creates opportunities for investments that can grow your wealth over time. Cultivating good saving habits early on can make a significant difference in achieving your long-term financial goals.

Begin by setting up automatic transfers to your savings account whenever you receive income. Even if it's a small amount, consistent saving will accumulate over time. As your income grows, consider increasing your savings contributions accordingly.

Create specific savings goals, such as saving for a dream vacation, purchasing a car, or building an emergency fund. Having tangible objectives will motivate you to save regularly and avoid dipping into your savings for non-essential expenses.

Seeking Financial Education

Financial education is a valuable tool for enhancing your money management skills. Keep an open mind and look for ways to increase your financial literacy. Read books, attend workshops, and follow reputable financial websites to stay informed about personal finance topics.

Additionally, consider taking courses on financial literacy or economics if available in your school or community. Many online platforms offer free or affordable courses that cover various aspects of money management. Learning about investing, budgeting, and money-saving strategies will empower you to make informed decisions about your finances.

Conclusion

Understanding the basics of money management is the first step towards financial independence and success. By creating a personal budget, tracking expenses and income, prioritizing emergency savings, and finding the right balance between income and expenses, you lay the groundwork for a solid financial future.

Remember that mastering money management is an ongoing journey. Be patient with yourself as you learn and apply these principles to your daily life. With financial discipline, responsible debt management, good saving habits, and continuous education, you will build the skills and confidence needed to navigate the complexities of personal finance successfully.

In the subsequent chapters of this e-book, we will delve deeper into various aspects of smart money moves for teens and young adults. Let's continue this journey together, equipping you with the knowledge and tools to make wise financial decisions and achieve your financial dreams.

Chapter Two

Budgeting Like a Pro

Budgeting is the cornerstone of effective money management. It empowers you to take control of your finances, allocate your income wisely, and achieve your financial goals. In this chapter, we will explore different budgeting methods, including the popular 50/30/20 rule and zero-based budgeting. Additionally, we'll discuss the importance of allocating funds for savings and investments and provide valuable tips for sticking to your budget consistently.

Exploring Different Budgeting Methods

Budgeting is not a one-size-fits-all approach; different methods suit various lifestyles and financial goals. It's essential to explore different budgeting techniques to find the one that aligns best with your needs and preferences.

1. **The 50/30/20 Rule:** This budgeting method involves dividing your after-tax income into three categories:

- **50% for Needs:** Allocate 50% of your income to cover essential expenses, such as rent, utilities, groceries, and transportation.

- **30% for Wants:** Dedicate 30% of your income to non-essential expenses, like dining out, entertainment, and shopping.

- **20% for Savings and Debt Repayment:** Reserve 20% of your income for savings, investments, and paying off debts.

2. **Zero-Based Budgeting:** With this method, you allocate every dollar of your income to various categories until you reach zero. In other words, your income minus your expenses, savings, and debt payments should equal zero. This approach encourages you to give every dollar a purpose, making it easier to track and manage your spending.

The 50/30/20 Rule

The 50/30/20 rule is a simple and effective budgeting method that provides a clear framework for managing your finances. By allocating specific percentages of your income to different categories, you can strike a balance between fulfilling your needs, enjoying your wants, and securing your financial future.

Step-by-Step Guide to Implementing the 50/30/20 Rule:

1. **Calculate Your After-Tax Income:** Begin by determining your monthly after-tax income—the amount you receive after taxes and other deductions.

2. **Allocate 50% to Needs:** Identify your essential expenses, including rent or mortgage, utilities, groceries, transportation, and insurance. Allocate 50% of your after-tax income to cover these necessary costs.

3. **Allocate 30% to Wants:** Your wants encompass discretionary expenses, such as dining out, entertainment, hobbies, and non-essential purchases. Use 30% of your income for these enjoyable but non-critical expenses.

4. **Allocate 20% to Savings and Debt Repayment:** The remaining 20% of your income should be dedicated to building savings and paying off debts. Establish an emergency fund, contribute to retirement accounts, and work towards becoming debt-free.

5. **Regularly Review and Adjust:** Budgeting is a dynamic process. Regularly review your spending habits, financial goals, and income changes. Adjust your budget as needed to ensure it reflects your current financial situation and priorities.

Zero-Based Budgeting

Zero-based budgeting is a proactive approach to money management. It encourages you to give every dollar a purpose, leaving no room for unaccounted expenses. This method can be especially helpful for those who want more control over their spending and wish to minimize unnecessary costs.

Step-by-Step Guide to Implementing Zero-Based Budgeting:

1. **Record your Income:** Start by listing all your income sources, such as salary, allowances, and any other money you receive.

2. **List your Expenses:** Create a comprehensive list of your expenses, including fixed costs like rent and utilities, variable expenses like groceries and entertainment, and debt payments.

3. **Allocate Funds:** Assign a specific amount to each expense category until your total allocations equal your after-tax income. Remember to prioritize essential expenses and allocate funds for savings and debt repayment.

4. **Track Your Spending:** Throughout the month, track your actual expenses and compare them to your budget allocations. You can make changes here and this will help you find areas where you could be overspending.

5. **Roll over Unspent Funds:** If you have money left in a category at the end of the month, consider rolling it over to the following month or reallocating it to other financial goals.

Allocating Funds for Savings and Investments

Setting aside a portion of your income for savings and investments is a critical step toward building wealth and achieving financial freedom. Saving money provides a safety net for emergencies and allows you to seize opportunities for growth and investment.

The Power of Compound Interest:

One of the most significant advantages of starting to save and invest early is the power of compound interest. Your financial resources can grow tremendously over time with compound interest. The longer you invest, the more your initial investment will generate, thanks to the interest earned on both your principal amount and accumulated interest.

Tips for Successful Saving and Investing:

1. **Automate Savings:** Set up automatic transfers to your savings and investment accounts. Automating the process ensures consistent contributions and removes the temptation to spend the money impulsively.

2. **Start Small and Be Consistent:** If you're new to saving and investing, start with a modest amount that you can comfortably set aside regularly. Gradually raise your contributions as your income rises.

3. **Diversify Your Investments:** Explore various investment options, such as stocks, bonds, mutual funds, and retirement accounts. Diversifying your portfolio helps spread risk and increases the potential for higher returns.

4. **Stay Informed:** Stay updated on financial news and market trends. While long-term investments benefit from a "set it and forget it" approach, it's

essential to be aware of economic changes that may impact your investment strategy.

Tips for Sticking to a Budget

Creating a budget is only the first step; sticking to it consistently is the key to successful money management. Here are some excellent pointers to keep you on course:

1. **Set Realistic Goals:** Establish achievable financial goals that motivate you to stick to your budget. Whether it's saving for a dream vacation or paying off student loans, having tangible objectives will keep you focused.

2. **Monitor Your Spending:** Regularly review your expenses to ensure they align with your budget. Identify areas where you may be overspending and find ways to cut back without sacrificing essential needs.

3. **Use Budgeting Apps:** Leverage technology to your advantage by using budgeting apps that help track your expenses, set financial goals, and send you reminders to stay within your budget.

4. **Involve Family or Friends:** If you share expenses with family or roommates, involve them in the budgeting process. Collaborate on setting financial goals and collectively commit to sticking to the budget.

5. **Practice Self-Discipline:** Avoid impulse spending by practicing self-discipline. Consider whether an expense is required and whether it is in line with your financial goals before making a purchase.

6. **Reward Yourself:** Celebrate your financial milestones and accomplishments. Treating yourself occasionally for sticking to your budget can be a powerful motivator to keep going.

Conclusion

Budgeting like a pro is essential for achieving financial success. By exploring different budgeting methods such as the 50/30/20 rule and zero-based budgeting, you can find the approach that suits your lifestyle and financial goals best. Allocating funds for savings and investments ensures you build a strong financial foundation for the future. Stay committed to your budget and use valuable tips to remain consistent in your money management journey.

In the following chapters, we will continue our exploration of smart money moves, delving into the world of saving and investing, credit management, and building a strong credit score. Remember, mastering money management takes time and practice, but the rewards of financial security and independence are well worth the effort.

Chapter Three

The Power of Saving and Investing

Saving and investing are two powerful tools that can pave the way to financial prosperity and security. In this chapter, we will explore the importance of saving regularly, the different types of savings accounts available, the basics of investments, and the various investment options such as stocks, bonds, and mutual funds. Additionally, we will discuss the concept of risk and return in investing, helping you make informed decisions to grow your wealth over time.

Importance of Saving Regularly

Regular saving is the key to successful money management. Whether you are setting aside a portion of your allowance or earnings from a part-time job, establishing a habit of consistent saving can lead to significant long-term benefits. Here's why saving regularly is essential:

1. Building an Emergency Fund:

Because of the unpredictability of life, unforeseen costs can occur at any time. An emergency fund provides a safety net to cover sudden medical bills, car repairs, or unexpected job loss without resorting to high-interest debt. Aim to have three to six months' worth of living expenses set aside in your emergency fund.

2. Securing Financial Freedom:

Saving regularly allows you to accumulate funds for future financial goals, such as buying a car, funding college education, or starting a business. By setting aside money consistently, you'll be better prepared to seize opportunities that come your way.

3. Taking Advantage of Compound Interest:

The power of compound interest is remarkable. As you save and invest, your money earns interest, and that interest can, in turn, earn more interest. Over time, compound interest can significantly grow your initial savings, making it a potent wealth-building tool.

4. Reducing Financial Stress:

Having savings cushions you against financial stress. It provides peace of mind, knowing that you have a financial buffer to handle unforeseen circumstances.

Types of Savings Accounts

When saving money, choosing the right savings account is crucial to make the most of your funds. Various types of savings accounts are available, each with its features and benefits. Here are common types of savings accounts:

1. Regular Savings Account:

A regular savings account is a basic account offered by banks and credit unions. It typically pays interest on your deposits, helping your money grow over time. Regular savings accounts provide easy access to your funds and are a suitable option for building an emergency fund.

2. High-Yield Savings Account:

An interest rate on a high-yield savings account is higher than one on a standard savings account. While the interest may not be substantial, it can help your savings grow faster. These accounts are usually offered by online banks and financial institutions.

3. Certificates of Deposit (CDs):

CDs are time-bound savings accounts with fixed terms, ranging from a few months to several years. In exchange for leaving your money untouched for the specified term, you receive a higher interest rate. CDs are ideal for long-term savings goals, but early withdrawals may incur penalties.

4. Money Market Accounts (MMAs):

Money market accounts combine the benefits of checking and savings accounts. They offer higher interest rates than regular savings accounts and may come with check-writing capabilities. MMAs are suitable for those who want easy access to their funds while earning a slightly higher interest rate.

Understanding Investments

Investing goes beyond saving money in traditional bank accounts. While saving is essential for short-term goals and emergencies, investing focuses on growing your wealth over the long term. Investments come with some level of risk, but they offer the potential for higher returns than traditional savings accounts.

Before delving into specific investment options, it's crucial to understand the basics of investments:

1. Risk and Return:

Investing involves taking on risk with the expectation of receiving a return on your investment. Generally speaking, the risk involved increases with possible gain. Different investment options carry different levels of risk, and understanding your risk tolerance is crucial in creating a balanced investment portfolio.

2. Diversification:

To lower risk, diversification is a strategy that involves distributing your investments across several asset classes and businesses. By diversifying your portfolio, you are less likely to experience significant losses if one investment performs poorly.

3. Time Horizon:

Your investment time horizon refers to the length of time you plan to invest before needing the money for a specific goal. Longer investment horizons allow you to take on more risk and potentially pursue higher-return investments.

4. Compound Growth:

Similar to compound interest in savings, compound growth in investing allows your investment earnings to generate additional earnings over time. Reinvesting dividends and capital gains can significantly boost your investment portfolio.

Stocks, Bonds, and Mutual Funds

Now that you understand the fundamentals of investing, let's explore some common investment options:

1. Stocks:

You purchase a share of ownership in a corporation when you buy stock. As a shareholder, you have the potential to benefit from the company's growth and profitability.

Stock prices can fluctuate based on market conditions and the company's performance.

2. Bonds:

Governments or businesses may issue bonds as a form of debt security. By purchasing a bond, you essentially lend money to the issuer in return for regular interest payments and the repayment of the principle amount when the bond matures. In comparison to stocks, bonds are typically regarded as lower-risk investments.

3. Mutual Funds:

A diverse portfolio of stocks, bonds, and other assets is purchased by mutual funds by pooling the money from numerous participants. Professional fund managers manage mutual funds, making them a convenient option for investors who prefer a hands-off approach.

4. Exchange-Traded Funds (ETFs):

Similar to mutual funds, ETFs also offer diversified investment portfolios. ETFs, on the other hand, offer flexibility and liquidity to investors by trading on stock markets like individual equities.

Risk and Return in Investing

Investing always involves an element of risk. The risk-return relationship dictates that higher-risk investments have the potential for higher returns, while lower-risk investments typically offer lower returns.

Types of Investment Risk:

1. **Market Risk:** The risk of investments declining in value due to economic, political, or market factors.

2. **Interest Rate Risk:** The risk of changes in interest rates affecting the value of fixed-income securities like bonds.

3. **Credit Risk:** The risk of a borrower failing to meet their debt obligations, resulting in potential losses for bondholders.

4. **Inflation Risk:** The risk that inflation will erode the purchasing power of your investments over time.

Mitigating Risk:

While it's impossible to eliminate all investment risk, there are ways to mitigate it:

1. **Diversification:** As mentioned earlier, spreading your investments across various asset classes and industries can reduce the impact of individual investment performance on your overall portfolio.

2. **Long-Term Perspective:** Maintaining a long-term investment horizon allows you to weather short-term market fluctuations and benefit from the power of compound growth.

3. **Understanding Risk Tolerance:** Assess your risk tolerance carefully to ensure your investments align with your comfort level. Avoid taking on more risk than you can handle emotionally or financially.

4. **Seeking Professional Advice:** If you're unsure about your investment choices, consider seeking advice from a qualified financial advisor. They can help create a personalized investment strategy based on your goals and risk tolerance.

Conclusion

Investing and saving are effective methods for increasing wealth and accomplishing financial goals. Saving regularly helps you establish financial security and create a safety net for emergencies. By understanding different types of savings accounts and investment options, you can make informed decisions that align with your financial objectives.

As you embark on your investment journey, remember that investing involves risk, and it's essential to develop a clear understanding of your risk tolerance and long-term objectives. By staying informed, diversifying your investments, and maintaining a long-term perspective, you'll be on your way to harnessing the power of saving and investing to secure a bright financial future.

Chapter Four

Navigating Credit Cards and Loans

In today's financial landscape, credit cards and loans play a significant role in our lives. Understanding how credit cards work and managing loans responsibly is essential for building a solid financial foundation. In this chapter, we will explore the ins and outs of credit cards, building credit responsibly, managing credit card debt, and the different types of loans available. Additionally, we will discuss interest rates and loan terms, equipping you with the knowledge to navigate credit and loans wisely.

How Credit Cards Work

A credit card is a financial tool that allows you to borrow money from a credit card issuer to make purchases. Unlike a debit card, which draws funds directly from your bank account, a credit card provides a line of credit that you can use up to a pre-approved limit. Here's how credit cards work:

1. **Credit Limit:** Each credit card comes with a credit limit, which is the maximum amount you can

charge on the card. The credit card issuer determines your credit limit based on factors such as your credit history, income, and debt-to-income ratio.

2. **Billing Cycle:** Credit card transactions occur within a billing cycle, typically a month long. Throughout this period, you can make purchases up to your credit limit.

3. **Minimum Payment:** At the end of each billing cycle, you will receive a credit card statement with a minimum payment due. Usually a small portion of your entire balance is used as this minimum payment. Paying the minimum amount by the due date will keep your account in good standing, but it's advisable to pay more to avoid accumulating high-interest charges.

4. **Interest Charges:** If you carry a balance on your credit card from one billing cycle to the next, you will be charged interest on the remaining balance. The interest rate, also known as the Annual

Percentage Rate (APR), varies based on your creditworthiness and the credit card issuer's terms.

Building Credit Responsibly

Credit cards are not only a convenient payment method but also an opportunity to build and establish credit history. Responsible credit card usage is essential for maintaining a positive credit score. Here's how you can build credit responsibly:

1. **Pay on Time:** Always pay your credit card bills on or before the due date. Late payments can negatively impact your credit score and may lead to late payment fees and increased interest rates.

2. **Keep Utilization Low:** Credit utilization refers to the percentage of your credit limit that you are currently using. Aim to keep your credit card utilization below 30% to demonstrate responsible credit management.

3. **Avoid Maxing Out:** Maxing out your credit card or consistently carrying high balances can harm your credit score and make it difficult to manage debt.

4. **Monitor Your Credit:** Regularly check your credit report to ensure accuracy and identify any errors or fraudulent activity. Equifax, Experian, and TransUnion, the three major credit bureaus, are required to provide you with a free credit report once a year.

Managing Credit Card Debt

Credit card debt can quickly become overwhelming if not managed carefully. If you find yourself struggling with credit card debt, consider the following strategies to regain control:

1. **Create a Repayment Plan:** Outline a clear repayment plan for your credit card debt. Prioritize paying off high-interest cards first while making at least the minimum payments on other cards.

2. **Consolidate Debt:** If you have multiple credit card debts with high-interest rates, consider consolidating them into a single loan with a lower interest rate. Debt consolidation can make it easier

to manage payments and potentially save on interest charges.

3. **Avoid New Debt:** While repaying credit card debt, avoid accruing new debt. Put a pause on unnecessary purchases and focus on your debt repayment plan.

4. **Negotiate with Creditors:** If you're facing financial hardship, contact your creditors to discuss possible options. Some may be willing to negotiate reduced interest rates or work out a repayment plan.

Types of Loans: Student Loans, Personal Loans, etc.

Loans are a common means of financing significant expenses, such as education, home purchases, or emergencies. Understanding the different types of loans can help you make informed decisions about borrowing:

1. **Student Loans:** Student loans are designed to finance higher education expenses. Federal student loans are those made available by the government, and private student loans are those made available by private lenders. Federal student loans often have

more favorable terms, including fixed interest rates and flexible repayment options.

2. **Personal Loans:** Personal loans are unsecured loans that can be used for various purposes, such as consolidating debt, covering medical expenses, or funding a special event. Both the interest rate and the payback conditions on personal loans are usually fixed.

3. **Auto Loans:** Auto loans are a type of financing that are used to buy a car. The car itself acts as security for the loan. Auto loans come with fixed interest rates and repayment terms.

4. **Mortgages:** A mortgage is a loan used to purchase a home. Mortgages have longer repayment terms (often 15 or 30 years) and may have fixed or adjustable interest rates.

Interest Rates and Loan Terms

The cost of borrowing is greatly affected by interest rates and loan conditions. Here's what you need to know about interest rates and loan terms:

1. **Interest Rates:** The cost of borrowing money, stated as a percentage of the loan amount, is the interest rate. Interest rates can be fixed (remain the same throughout the loan term) or adjustable (fluctuate based on market conditions).

2. **Annual Percentage Rate (APR):** The APR includes the interest rate and any additional fees or charges associated with the loan. Comparing APRs can help you determine the overall cost of different loan offers.

3. **Loan Terms:** The time frame for loan repayment is referred to as the loan terms. Shorter loan terms usually come with higher monthly payments but lower overall interest costs.

Conclusion

Credit cards and loans can be valuable financial tools if used responsibly. Understanding how credit cards work, building credit responsibly, and managing credit card debt are essential for maintaining a positive credit history. When considering loans, research the different types available, and carefully assess interest rates and loan terms.

As you navigate the world of credit and loans, remember that responsible borrowing can enhance your financial opportunities, while imprudent decisions may lead to financial challenges. By making informed choices and staying disciplined in your financial decisions, you can build a strong credit profile and use credit and loans to your advantage.

Chapter Five

Building a Strong Credit Score

A critical component of your financial life is your credit score. It is a numerical representation of your creditworthiness and impacts your ability to obtain loans, credit cards, and other financial opportunities. Building and maintaining a strong credit score is essential for achieving financial success. In this chapter, we will explore what a credit score is, the factors that affect credit scores, strategies for building and maintaining good credit, checking and improving your credit report, and how to deal with credit score errors.

What is a Credit Score?

A credit score is a three-digit number that ranges from 300 to 850, serving as a summary of your credit history and financial behavior. It is calculated based on the information in your credit report, which includes your credit accounts, payment history, outstanding debts, and other credit-related data. Lenders and creditors use your credit score to assess your credit risk and determine whether to approve your loan or credit application.

FICO® scores and VantageScore® are the two most widely utilized credit scoring models. These scores are calculated using complex algorithms that weigh various factors to produce a single numerical value representing your creditworthiness.

Factors Affecting Credit Scores

Your credit score is impacted by numerous factors. You may make smart choices to increase your creditworthiness by being aware of the following factors:

1. **Payment History:** Your payment history is the most significant factor in calculating your credit score. Consistently paying on time displays prudent credit conduct.

2. **Credit Utilization:** The amount of available credit that is currently being used, expressed as a percentage. Keeping your credit utilization below 30% is generally considered favorable for your credit score.

3. **Credit History Length:** The length of your credit history matters. An extended credit history illustrates your capacity to responsibly manage credit over time.

4. **Credit Mix:** Having a diverse mix of credit accounts, such as credit cards, loans, and retail accounts, can positively impact your credit score.

5. **New Credit Applications:** Applying for multiple credit accounts within a short period can negatively affect your credit score. A little amount of your score may be impacted by each credit query.

Strategies for Building and Maintaining Good Credit

Building and maintaining good credit requires responsible financial habits and consistent efforts. Here are some strategies to help you build and maintain a strong credit score:

1. **Pay on Time, Every Time:** Always make your payments on time. Create automatic or recurring payments to make sure you never forget a payment's due date.

2. **Keep Credit Card Balances Low:** Aim to keep your credit card balances well below your credit limits. High credit card balances can hurt your credit utilization and, subsequently, your credit score.

3. **Avoid Opening Too Many New Accounts:** Opening multiple credit accounts within a short period can signal to creditors that you may be seeking credit urgently, potentially affecting your credit score negatively.

4. **Use Credit Responsibly:** Use credit cards and loans responsibly, only borrowing what you can afford to repay. Avoid maxing out credit cards or taking on more debt than necessary.

5. **Keep Old Accounts Open:** The length of your credit history matters, so try to keep older credit accounts open even if you don't use them frequently.

Checking and Improving Your Credit Report

Regularly checking your credit report is crucial for monitoring your credit health and identifying potential errors or fraudulent activity. Each of the three main credit bureaus—Equifax, Experian, and TransUnion—is required to provide you with one free credit report each year. Here's how to check and improve your credit report:

1. **Review Your Credit Report:** Obtain your free credit reports and review them carefully for any inaccuracies or suspicious activity. Any mistakes you discover should be disputed with the credit bureau so they can be fixed.

2. **Report Fraudulent Activity:** If you notice unauthorized accounts or transactions on your credit report, report them immediately to the credit bureaus and the respective creditors.

3. **Monitor Your Accounts:** Regularly review your credit card and loan statements to ensure all transactions are legitimate. Report any unauthorized charges to your card issuer promptly.

4. **Stay Informed:** Educate yourself about credit management and how different actions can impact

your credit score. Knowledge is power when it comes to building and maintaining good credit.

Dealing with Credit Score Errors

Errors on your credit report can have a significant impact on your credit score and overall financial health. If you discover errors on your credit report, take the following steps to address them:

1. **File a Dispute:** If you find inaccuracies on your credit report, file a dispute with the credit bureau(s) reporting the error. In support of your claim, provide evidence.

2. **Follow Up:** Follow up with the credit bureau to ensure they investigate your dispute thoroughly and make necessary corrections.

3. **Notify Creditors:** If the error involves a specific creditor, notify them of the mistake and provide any evidence supporting your claim.

4. **Be Patient:** Resolving credit report errors may take time, so be patient throughout the process.

Regularly check your credit report to confirm that the corrections have been made.

Conclusion

Building and maintaining a strong credit score is a critical aspect of personal finance. Your credit score can open doors to better financial opportunities and lower interest rates on loans and credit cards. By understanding the factors that affect your credit score, adopting responsible credit practices, regularly monitoring your credit report, and addressing any errors promptly, you can build a positive credit history and secure a stable financial future.

Chapter Six

Smart Ways to Pay for College

Pursuing higher education is a valuable investment in your future, but the costs associated with college can be significant. Fortunately, there are various smart ways to finance your college education without burdening yourself with overwhelming debt. In this chapter, we will explore the different methods of paying for college, including understanding college costs, scholarships and grants, federal financial aid, work-study programs, and the responsible use of student loans.

Understanding College Costs

Before diving into financing options, it's essential to have a clear understanding of the costs associated with attending college. College expenses go beyond tuition fees and can include:

1. **Tuition and Fees:** The core cost of attending college includes tuition fees, which vary depending on the institution and the program of study.

2. **Room and Board:** If you plan to live on-campus, room and board expenses cover your housing and meal plans. Off-campus students need to consider rent and food costs.

3. **Books and Supplies:** Course materials, textbooks, and supplies can add to the overall cost of your education.

4. **Transportation:** Commuting to campus or traveling home during breaks comes with transportation expenses.

5. **Personal Expenses:** Miscellaneous expenses for personal items and leisure activities are also part of college living costs.

6. **Health Insurance:** Some colleges require students to have health insurance coverage.

Scholarships and Grants

Scholarships and grants are excellent sources of free money for college that do not need to be repaid. These financial awards are based on various criteria, such as academic achievements, talents, community service, or specific demographics. Here's how to find and secure scholarships and grants:

1. **Research Scholarship Opportunities:** Look for scholarships offered by colleges, private organizations, community groups, and government agencies. Many online platforms also aggregate scholarship opportunities based on different criteria.

2. **Apply Early and Often:** Apply for as many scholarships as you are eligible for. The more applications you submit, the higher your chances of receiving financial aid.

3. **Focus on Local Scholarships:** Local scholarships often have fewer applicants, increasing your likelihood of winning.

4. **Highlight Your Achievements:** Showcase your achievements, talents, and extracurricular activities in scholarship applications to stand out as a strong candidate.

5. **Maintain Academic Performance:** Many scholarships require students to maintain a certain GPA, so continue to excel academically.

Federal Financial Aid

Federal financial aid includes grants, work-study programs, and federal student loans offered by the U.S. Department of Education. The Free Application for Federal Student Aid (FAFSA) must be filled out in order to submit a request for federal funding. Here are the key components of federal financial aid:

1. **Grants:** Federal grants, such as the Pell Grant, are need-based awards that do not require repayment.

2. **Work-Study Programs:** Work-study programs provide part-time job opportunities on campus or with approved off-campus employers to help students earn money for their education.

3. **Federal Student Loans:** Federal student loans offer lower interest rates and more flexible repayment options compared to private loans. While they need to be repaid, federal student loans

offer various repayment plans based on income and financial circumstances.

Work-Study Programs

Work-study programs are an excellent way to earn money while attending college. These programs offer part-time employment on or off-campus, typically related to your field of study or community service. Work-study benefits include:

1. **Financial Assistance:** Earning money through a work-study job can help cover college expenses and reduce reliance on loans.

2. **Work Experience:** Work-study jobs often provide valuable work experience and skill development, enhancing your resume after graduation.

3. **Flexible Scheduling:** Employers understand the importance of academics and usually offer flexible work schedules to accommodate your classes.

4. **Networking Opportunities:** Work-study jobs can help you build professional connections that may lead to future job opportunities.

Responsible Use of Student Loans

While scholarships, grants, and work-study programs can significantly reduce the need for student loans, borrowing may still be necessary for some students. If you take out student loans, it's crucial to do so responsibly:

1. **Borrow Only What You Need:** Only borrow the amount necessary to cover essential college expenses, such as tuition, fees, and living costs.

2. **Understand Loan Terms:** Familiarize yourself with the terms and conditions of your loans, including interest rates, repayment options, and grace periods.

3. **Consider Federal Loans First:** Federal student loans often offer more favorable terms and protections compared to private loans. Before going to private lenders, explore all federal loan possibilities.

4. **Budget for Repayment:** Create a budget for your post-graduation finances to ensure you can comfortably manage loan repayment along with other living expenses.

5. **Explore Loan Forgiveness and Repayment Assistance Programs:** Some professions and public service careers offer loan forgiveness or repayment assistance programs. Research options related to your career path.

Conclusion

Paying for college requires careful planning and consideration of the available financial aid options. Understanding college costs, seeking scholarships and grants, and exploring federal financial aid and work-study opportunities can significantly reduce the financial burden of higher education. If you need to borrow student loans, do so responsibly and be mindful of your future financial obligations.

By combining these smart approaches to finance your education, you can build a strong foundation for a

successful academic journey without compromising your
financial well-being.

Chapter Seven

Entrepreneurship and Making Money

In the pursuit of financial independence and success, entrepreneurship offers a path filled with opportunities and rewards. Starting and running a business allows you to unleash your creativity, identify your passion and skills, and make money doing what you love. In this chapter, we will explore the world of entrepreneurship, including exploring entrepreneurship opportunities, identifying your passion and skills, starting and running a business, marketing and sales strategies, and financial management tips for entrepreneurs.

Exploring Entrepreneurship Opportunities

Entrepreneurship is about identifying gaps in the market and finding innovative solutions to meet the needs of customers. Here's how you can explore entrepreneurship opportunities:

1. **Market Research:** Conduct thorough market research to identify areas with demand but limited

supply. Look for problems that people face daily and think about potential solutions.

2. **Analyze Trends:** Stay informed about industry trends and emerging technologies. Spotting trends early can open up exciting entrepreneurial ventures.

3. **Observe Your Passions:** Pay attention to your interests and hobbies. Sometimes, your passion can lead to unique business ideas.

4. **Network and Collaborate:** Attend industry events, networking sessions, and entrepreneurship conferences to meet like-minded individuals and explore potential collaborations.

Identifying Your Passion and Skills

Entrepreneurship thrives on passion and skills. Identify what drives you and your unique capabilities to build a business that aligns with who you are. Here's how to identify your passion and skills:

1. **Self-Reflection:** Spend some time thinking about your passions, principles, and what makes you happy. Consider the pursuits that cause you to get idly distracted.

2. **Assess Your Skills:** Identify your strengths and weaknesses. Focus on leveraging your strengths to build a business around your core competencies.

3. **Seek Feedback:** Ask friends, family, or mentors for honest feedback about your skills and areas where they believe you excel.

4. **Experiment and Learn:** Don't be afraid to try new things and learn from your experiences. The journey of self-discovery is a valuable part of the entrepreneurial process.

Starting and Running a Business

Once you've identified your entrepreneurial opportunity and passion, it's time to turn your idea into a tangible business. Here are the essential steps to start and run a business:

1. **Create a Business Plan:** Outline your business idea, target market, products or services, marketing strategies, and financial projections in a comprehensive business plan.

2. **Choose a Legal Structure:** Choose your company's legal structure, such as a corporation, limited liability company (LLC), partnership, or sole proprietorship.

3. **Register Your Business:** Register your business with the appropriate government authorities and obtain any necessary licenses and permits.

4. **Build Your Team:** If your business requires additional manpower, recruit individuals who share your vision and can contribute to your venture's success.

5. **Develop Your Product or Service:** To satisfy the demands of your target market, improve your product or service. A successful business depends on providing high-quality products and gratifying customers.

6. **Set up Financial Systems:** To keep track of revenue, costs, and profits, implement reliable financial systems. As a way to simplify financial administration, think about employing accounting software.

7. **Comply with Regulations:** Familiarize yourself with business regulations, tax obligations, and other legal requirements related to your industry.

Marketing and Sales Strategies

Marketing and sales strategies are vital for attracting customers and driving revenue for your business. Here are some effective marketing and sales techniques:

1. **Know Your Target Market:** Understand your target customers' needs, preferences, and pain points to tailor your marketing messages accordingly.

2. **Build a Strong Online Presence:** Establish a professional website and leverage social media platforms to reach a wider audience.

3. **Content Marketing:** Create valuable and engaging content, such as blog posts, videos, or podcasts, to showcase your expertise and attract potential customers.

4. **Networking and Partnerships:** Network with other entrepreneurs, influencers, and industry leaders. Collaborate on projects or cross-promote each other's businesses to expand your reach.

5. **Offer Promotions and Discounts:** Entice customers with limited-time promotions, discounts, or loyalty programs to encourage repeat business.

6. **Customer Feedback and Reviews:** Encourage customers to provide feedback and reviews, as positive testimonials can boost your credibility.

Financial Management for Entrepreneurs

Sound financial management is essential for the long-term success of your business. Here are some financial management tips for entrepreneurs:

1. **Separate Personal and Business Finances:** Maintain separate bank accounts and credit cards for your personal and business expenses.

2. **Create a Budget:** Develop a budget that outlines your expected income and expenses. Monitor your actual financial performance against the budget regularly.

3. **Manage Cash Flow:** Keep a close eye on your cash flow to ensure you have enough funds to cover operating expenses and investments.

4. **Plan for Taxes:** Set aside a portion of your earnings for taxes. Consult with an accountant to understand your tax obligations and potential deductions.

5. **Save for Emergencies:** Build an emergency fund to handle unexpected expenses or downturns in your business.

6. **Invest in Growth:** Allocate a portion of your profits to invest in the growth and expansion of your business.

Conclusion

The journey of entrepreneurship is one of excitement, possibilities, and challenges. By exploring entrepreneurship opportunities, identifying your passion and skills, starting and running a business, employing effective marketing and sales strategies, and practicing sound financial management, you can build a successful and rewarding entrepreneurial venture. Embrace the journey, learn from your experiences, and continue to innovate to achieve your entrepreneurial dreams.

Chapter Eight

The Importance of Giving Back

While achieving financial success is important, it's equally crucial to recognize the impact we can make on others and our communities through charitable giving and giving back. Giving back not only benefits those in need but also enriches our lives in meaningful ways. In this chapter, we will explore the significance of giving to others, incorporating charitable giving into your financial plan, volunteering and community involvement, creating a positive social impact, and the joy of giving.

Benefits of Giving to Others

Giving to others goes beyond financial contributions; it involves sharing our time, skills, and resources to make a positive difference in the lives of others. The benefits of giving back are profound and extend to both the recipients and the givers:

1. **Sense of Purpose:** Giving back provides a sense of purpose and fulfillment as we contribute to causes that align with our values.

2. **Strengthening Communities:** Charitable giving strengthens communities by addressing critical needs and fostering a sense of unity and support.

3. **Social Connection:** Engaging in philanthropy and giving back connects us with like-minded individuals who share similar passions and values.

4. **Personal Growth:** Volunteering and giving provide opportunities for personal growth, skill development, and gaining new perspectives.

Incorporating Charitable Giving into Your Financial Plan

Incorporating charitable giving into your financial plan ensures that you can contribute to causes you care about without compromising your financial stability. Here are some strategies to make giving a part of your financial journey:

1. **Set Giving Goals:** Determine how much you want to give annually or monthly, and include it as a line item in your budget.

2. **Choose Causes Close to Your Heart:** Select charities or causes that resonate with your values and interests.

3. **Automate Donations:** Set up automatic contributions to your chosen charities to ensure consistent giving.

4. **Maximize Tax Benefits:** If you itemize deductions, explore potential tax benefits for your charitable contributions.

Volunteering and Community Involvement

Beyond financial contributions, volunteering and community involvement allow you to make a direct impact on the lives of others. Consider these benefits of volunteering:

1. **Hands-On Experience:** Volunteering offers hands-on experience and a deeper understanding of the challenges faced by those in need.

2. **Building Empathy:** Engaging with different communities and individuals cultivates empathy and compassion.

3. **Skill Development:** Volunteering can help you develop new skills or apply existing skills in unique ways.

4. **Networking Opportunities:** Volunteering connects you with people from diverse backgrounds and expands your network.

Creating a Positive Social Impact

Giving back contributes to creating a positive social impact and addressing pressing social issues. By supporting organizations and initiatives that focus on education, poverty alleviation, healthcare, environmental sustainability, and other vital areas, you become part of a collective effort to drive positive change.

The Joy of Giving

The joy of giving lies in the heartfelt satisfaction of making a difference, no matter how big or small. Here's what the joy of giving can bring into your life:

1. **Gratitude:** Witnessing the impact of your giving can evoke a profound sense of gratitude for your own blessings.

2. **Happiness and Fulfillment:** Giving back often leads to increased happiness and a sense of fulfillment in life.

3. **Inspiring Others:** Your acts of giving can inspire others to do the same, creating a ripple effect of kindness and generosity.

4. **Legacy of Giving:** Building a legacy of giving sets an example for future generations to embrace philanthropy.

Conclusion

As you focus on building your financial future, remember the importance of giving back and making a positive impact on others and the world around you. Whether through financial contributions, volunteering, or community involvement, giving back enriches your life and enhances the lives of those you touch. Embrace the joy of giving and the profound difference it can make in creating a more compassionate and caring society.

Chapter Nine

Making Sound Financial Decisions

Sound financial decision-making is essential for achieving financial security and long-term prosperity. As you navigate the complexities of personal finance, it's crucial to recognize and avoid financial scams, understand the importance of insurance, engage in long-term financial planning, secure your retirement savings and investments, and prepare for unexpected financial situations. In this chapter, we will explore these key aspects of making sound financial decisions.

Recognizing and Avoiding Financial Scams

Financial scams are designed to deceive individuals and exploit their financial vulnerabilities. Here's how to recognize and avoid falling victim to financial scams:

1. **Stay Informed:** Educate yourself about common types of financial scams, such as phishing emails, pyramid schemes, and investment fraud.

2. **Be Cautious of Unsolicited Offers:** Be skeptical of unsolicited phone calls, emails, or messages

promising financial opportunities that sound too good to be true.

3. **Protect Personal Information:** Never share sensitive financial information, such as social security numbers or bank account details, with unknown parties.

4. **Verify Credentials:** Before engaging in any financial transactions, verify the credentials of the individuals or companies involved.

5. **Report Suspicious Activities:** If you encounter a potential scam, report it to the appropriate authorities to protect others from falling victim.

Understanding Insurance: Health, Auto, and Life

Insurance is a vital component of financial protection, safeguarding against unexpected events that can lead to significant financial strain. Understand these key insurance types:

1. **Health Insurance:** Health insurance covers medical expenses, ensuring access to quality healthcare without incurring exorbitant costs.

2. **Auto Insurance:** Auto insurance provides financial protection in the event of an accident or damage to your vehicle.

3. **Life Insurance:** Life insurance offers financial support to beneficiaries in the event of the policyholder's death, providing peace of mind for loved ones.

Long-Term Financial Planning

Long-term financial planning involves setting financial goals and creating a roadmap to achieve them. Here's how to engage in effective long-term financial planning:

1. **Set Clear Goals:** Define your long-term financial goals, such as buying a home, saving for retirement, or starting a business.

2. **Create a Budget:** Develop a budget to track your income and expenses and ensure you are living within your means.

3. **Build an Emergency Fund:** Establish an emergency fund to cover unexpected expenses and financial setbacks.

4. **Invest for the Future:** Consider investment options that align with your risk tolerance and financial objectives.

5. **Review and Adjust:** Regularly review your financial plan and make adjustments as needed based on changes in your life or financial circumstances.

Retirement Savings and Investments

Preparing for retirement is a crucial aspect of sound financial decision-making. Ensure your retirement savings and investments are on track:

1. **Start Early:** Begin saving for retirement as early as possible to take advantage of compound interest and maximize your savings.

2. **Utilize Retirement Accounts:** Contribute to retirement accounts like 401(k)s or IRAs, taking advantage of any employer match.

3. **Diversify Investments:** Diversify your investment portfolio to spread risk and achieve long-term growth.

4. **Monitor Performance:** Regularly review the performance of your retirement investments and make adjustments when necessary.

Preparing for Unexpected Financial Situations

Life is unpredictable, and unexpected financial situations can arise at any time. Be prepared with these strategies:

1. **Emergency Fund:** Maintain an emergency fund equivalent to at least three to six months' worth of living expenses to handle unforeseen events.

2. **Insurance Coverage:** Ensure you have appropriate insurance coverage to protect against unexpected medical or property-related expenses.

3. **Estate Planning:** Establish an estate plan, including a will and power of attorney, to protect your assets and provide for your loved ones in the event of your incapacity or passing.

4. **Flexible Budgeting:** Create a flexible budget that allows you to adjust your spending when faced with unexpected financial challenges.

Conclusion

Making sound financial decisions is the foundation of a secure and prosperous future. By recognizing and avoiding financial scams, understanding the importance of insurance, engaging in long-term financial planning, securing retirement savings, and preparing for unexpected situations, you can build a strong financial foundation that will serve you well throughout your life journey. Take control of your financial well-being, stay informed, and make choices that align with your financial goals and values.

Chapter Ten

The Path to Financial Independence

Congratulations on completing the journey of "10 Smart Money Moves: Building Money Lessons for Teens and Young Adults." Throughout this e-book, we've explored essential money lessons that lay the groundwork for achieving financial independence. As we conclude this guide, let's recap the key money lessons, emphasize the importance of building a strong financial foundation, maintaining consistent financial habits, setting long-term financial goals, and ultimately, achieving financial independence.

Recap of Key Money Lessons

Before we embark on the path to financial independence, let's briefly recap the key money lessons covered in this e-book:

1. **Understanding the Basics of Money Management:** This chapter introduced the fundamental concepts of money management, including creating a personal budget, tracking

expenses and income, and the importance of emergency savings.

2. **Budgeting Like a Pro:** We explored different budgeting methods, such as the 50/30/20 rule and zero-based budgeting, and learned how to allocate funds for savings and investments while sticking to a budget.

3. **The Power of Saving and Investing:** This chapter emphasized the importance of regular saving, the different types of savings accounts, and an introduction to investments like stocks, bonds, and mutual funds.

4. **Navigating Credit Cards and Loans:** We learned how credit cards work, the responsible use of credit, and the management of credit card debt. Additionally, we explored various types of loans and their impact on financial well-being.

5. **Building a Strong Credit Score:** This chapter delved into understanding credit scores, the factors

that affect them, and strategies for building and maintaining a good credit score.

6. **Entrepreneurship and Making Money:** We explored the world of entrepreneurship, identifying passion and skills, starting and running a business, and the joy of giving back.

7. **Making Sound Financial Decisions:** Understanding insurance, long-term financial planning, retirement savings, and preparing for unexpected financial situations were key highlights of this chapter.

Building a Strong Financial Foundation

To achieve financial independence, it is essential to build a strong financial foundation. This involves adopting healthy financial habits, avoiding debt traps, and living within your means. A strong financial foundation sets the stage for future growth and enables you to navigate financial challenges with confidence.

Importance of Consistency in Financial Habits

Consistency is the key to success in any endeavor, including personal finance. Consistent financial habits, such as saving regularly, avoiding unnecessary expenses, and making on-time payments, contribute to long-term financial stability and growth. It's the small daily actions that add up to significant financial progress over time.

Setting Long-Term Financial Goals

Financial independence requires a clear vision and long-term financial goals. Setting specific, measurable, achievable, relevant, and time-bound (SMART) goals empowers you to stay focused and motivated. Whether your goals involve buying a home, funding education, or retiring early, a well-defined plan guides you on the path to success.

Achieving Financial Independence

Financial independence is the stage where your income from investments, savings, and passive sources surpasses your expenses, giving you the freedom to live life on your terms. The road to financial independence is one that calls for commitment, self-control, and persistence. By following the money lessons outlined in this e-book, you have already taken significant steps toward this goal.

Conclusion

As we conclude "10 Smart Money Moves: Building Money Lessons for Teens and Young Adults," remember that building a strong financial foundation, maintaining consistent financial habits, setting long-term financial goals, and striving for financial independence are lifelong pursuits. Embrace the knowledge and principles shared in this e-book, and continue learning and growing in your financial journey.

Financial independence is within reach, and with determination, dedication, and a commitment to sound money management, you can create a secure and prosperous future for yourself. Congratulations on your commitment to financial success, and may your journey toward financial independence be filled with success, happiness, and peace of mind.